Happily Forever After

WORDS OF ADVICE FOR MARRIED COUPLES

Happily Forever After

WORDS OF ADVICE FOR MARRIED COUPLES

by

MICHELE ASHMAN BELL

with

ERIKA BRENDLE, LINDSAY GARDNER,
ALICIA GUBLER, AND NICOLE MILLER

ISBN: 978-1-932898-68-2
e. 1

Published by:
Spring Creek Book Company
P.O. Box 50355
Provo, Utah 84605-0355

www.springcreekbooks.com

Cover design © Spring Creek Book Company
Cover design by Nicole Cunningham

Printed in the United States of America
10 9 8 7 6 5 4 3 2 1

Printed on acid-free paper

This book is dedicated to our husbands and children, to our parents Nolan and Yvonne Ashman, and our grandparents, Albert and Noreen Ashman, and Ernest and Viola Bauer.

FOREWORD

While giving a wedding shower for a dear friend, I requested those who attended bring a piece of advice they could share with this bride-to-be. I was astounded as I listened to the words of counsel and wisdom shared that day and wished that I had taken time to write down the many wonderful thoughts and advice.

Since then, my sisters and I have gathered advice on marriage from our prophets and church leaders and from a vast array of people; old, young, newlywed, oldeywed, some who have lost a spouse, or were in a marriage that didn't work out. Some have been Bishops, Stake Presidents, Relief Society Presidents, Primary Presidents and Young Men or Young Women Presidents. Most importantly, all of them are temple worthy and have similar goals to achieve an ideal marriage that can last through the eternities, a marriage in which couples can live . . . happily forever after.

Michele Ashman Bell

TABLE OF CONTENTS

Commitment

Commitment is dedication or loyalty to a principle, person, or institution. This loyalty does not waver but remains constant regardless of the situation. Commitment is a binding force in a good marriage. Emotions come and go. One day we may see the person we love as all things perfect and desirable. Another day irritations or conflicts may bring us to the point of dislike for the same person.

Emotions may fluctuate, but loyalty does not. If commitment is firm, we do not give up or desert a relationship when adverse circumstances occur.

Marriage relationships can be enriched by better communication. One important way is to pray together. This will resolve many of the differences, if there are any, between the couple before sleep comes.

JAMES E. FAUST

"The Enriching of Marriage," *Ensign*, Nov. 1977, p. 9.

The marriage that is based upon selfishness is almost certain to fail. The one who marries for wealth or the one who marries for prestige or social plane is certain to be disappointed. The one who marries to satisfy vanity and pride or who marries to spite or to show up another person is fooling only himself.

But the one who marries to give happiness as well as receive it, to give service as well as to receive it, and who looks after the interests of the two and then the family as it comes will have a good chance that the marriage will be a happy one.

SPENCER W. KIMBALL

Address at Brigham Young University, September 7, 1976.

Therefore shall a man leave his father and his mother, and shall cleave unto his wife, and they shall be one flesh.

GENESIS 2:24

No combination of power can destroy marriage except the power within either or both of the spouses themselves.

SPENCER W. KIMBALL

Marriage and Divorce, Deseret Book, p. 17.

First, am I able to think of the interest of my marriage and partner first before I think of my own desires?

Second, how deep is my commitment to my companion, aside from any other interests?

Third, is he or she my best friend?

Fourth, do I have respect for the dignity of my partner as a person of worth and value?

Fifth, do we quarrel over money? Money itself seems neither to make a couple happy, nor the lack of it, necessarily, to make them unhappy, but money is often a symbol of selfishness.

Sixth, is there a spiritually sanctifying bond between us?

JAMES E. FAUST

Ensign, Nov. 1977, p. 10.

Communication

The best and most effective time to be concerned about conflicts over the basic principles that bring happiness to marriage is before the decision to enter into marriage is made. Some of the greatest tragedies occur because of decisions made largely on whimsical, emotional impulses.

Every successful marriage requires much selfless effort and adjustment on the part of both partners. The more ideals and fundamental purposes in life that are held in common by the husband and wife, the more likelihood of success in their marriage. When differences exist, they can become a source of constant or recurring stress and contention.

DEAN L. LARSEN

Ensign, Sept. 1982, p.59.

Even under the best of conditions, marriage involves the merging of two sets of free agency, two sets of family traditions, two sets of personal habits, preferences, attitudes, and beliefs. But this process of symbolically becoming one by becoming like-minded does not occur through merely living in the same house. Husbands and wives must be willing to share their innermost thoughts, needs, desires, hopes, and dreams with each other.

SPENCER J. CONDIE

Ensign, July 1986, pp. 54-55.

It seems to me that communication is essentially a matter of talking with one another. Let that talk be quiet for quiet talk is the language of love. It is the language of peace. It is the language of God. It is when we raise our voices that tiny mole hills of indifference become mountains of conflict. . . .

The voice of heaven is a still small voice. The voice of peace in the home is a quiet voice.

There is need for much discipline in marriage, not of one's companion but of one's self. Husbands, wives, remember, "He [or she] that is slow to anger is better than the mighty." (Proverbs 16:32)

Cultivate the art of the soft answer. It will bless your homes, it will bless your lives, it will bless your companionships, it will bless your children.

GORDON B. HINCKLEY

Cornerstones of a Happy Home, excerpt from Husbands and Wives Fireside, Jan. 29, 1984, audiovisual resource (OT181 or VH256).

Every couple, whether in the first or the twenty-first year of marriage, should discover the value of pillow-talk time at the end of the day—the perfect time to take inventory, to talk about tomorrow. And best of all, it's a time when love and appreciation for one another can be reconfirmed. The end of another day is also the perfect setting to say, "Sweetheart, I am sorry about what happened today. Please forgive me."

Since a husband and wife usually come into marriage with dissimilar backgrounds and perspectives, differences of opinion are almost inevitable, and conflict is difficult to avoid. Whether couples resolve their conflicts or not can depend on how well they communicate.

When their communication is designed to build each other, or at least not to tear down, the marriage can grow in healthy ways. But when communication is negative or nonexistent, the growth of the relationship can be stunted.

Priesthood leaders, marriage counselors, and others who help married couples resolve difficulties have long recognized these truths.

EDWIN O. HAROLDSEN &
BARRY L. JOHNSON

Ensign, Feb. 1993, p. 20.

11

Marriage relationships can be enriched by better communication. One important way is to pray together. This will resolve many of the differences, if there are any, between the couple before sleep comes. I do not mean to overemphasize differences, but they are real, and make things interesting.

Our differences are the little pinches of salt which can make the marriage seem sweeter. We communicate in a thousand ways, such as a smile, a brush of the hair, a gentle touch, and remembering each day to say, "I love you" and the husband to say, "You're beautiful." Some other important words to say, which appropriate, are "I'm sorry." Listening is excellent communication.

JAMES E. FAUST

Ensign, Nov. 1977, p. 9.

I hear so many complaints from men and women that they cannot communicate with one another. Perhaps I am naive, but I do not understand this. Communication is essentially a matter of conversation.

They must have communicated when they are courting. Can they not continue to speak together after marriage? Can they not discuss with one another in an open and frank and candid and happy way their interests, their problems, their challenges, their desires?

It seems to me that communication is largely a matter of talking with one another. But let that talk be quiet, for quiet talk is the language of love. It is the language of peace. It is the language of God. . . . The voice of heaven is a still small voice. The voice of peace in the home is a quiet voice.

GORDON B. HINCKLEY

'Cornerstones of a Happy Home,' Husbands and Wives
Fireside Satellite Broadcast, Jan. 29, 1984.

My husband and I had been married about two years—just long enough for me to realize that he was a normal man rather than a knight on a white charger—when I read a magazine article recommending that married couples schedule regular talks to discuss, truthfully and candidly, the habits or mannerisms they find annoying in each other.

We were to name five things we found annoying, and I started off. I told him that I didn't like the way he ate grapefruit. He peeled it and ate it like an orange! Nobody else I knew ate grapefruit like that. Could a girl be expected to spend a lifetime, and even eternity, watching her husband eat grapefruit like an orange?

After I finished with my five, it was his turn to tell the things he disliked about me. He said, "Well, to tell the truth, I can't think of anything I don't like about you, Honey."

Gasp.

I quickly turned my back, because I didn't know how to explain the tears that had filled my eyes and were running down my face.

Whenever I hear of married couples being incompatible, I always wonder if they are suffering from what I now call the Grapefruit Syndrome.

L O L A   B .   W A L T E R S

Ensign, Apr. 1993, p. 13.

Covenants

From the moment of birth into mortality to the time we are married in the temple, everything we have in the whole gospel system is to prepare and qualify us to enter that holy order of matrimony which makes us husband and wife in this life and in the world to come. . . . There is nothing in this world as important as the creation and perfection of family units.

BRUCE R. McCONKIE

Quoted in "The Family Is Central To The Creator's Plan," *Ensign*, Dec. 2004, p. 51.

If a man marry a wife not by me,
their covenant and marriage is
not of force when they are dead.

DOCTRINE AND COVENANTS 132: 15

In an eternal marriage, the thought of ending what began with a covenant between God and each other simply has little place. When challenges come and our individual weaknesses are revealed, the remedy is to repent, improve, and apologize, not to separate or divorce. When we make covenants with the Lord and our eternal companion, we should do everything in our power to honor the terms.

MARLIN K. JENSEN

Ensign, Oct. 1994, p. 47.

If a man marry a wife by my word, which is my law, and by the new and everlasting covenant, and it is sealed unto them by the Holy Spirit of promise, by him who is anointed, unto whom I have appointed this power and the keys of this priesthood . . . it shall be done unto them in all things whatsoever my servant hath put upon them, in time, and through all eternity; and shall be of full force when they are out of the world; and they shall pass by the angels, and the gods, which are set there, to their exaltation and glory in all things, as hath been sealed upon their heads.

DOCTRINE AND COVENANTS 132:19

Marriage itself must be regarded as a sacred covenant before God. A married couple have an obligation not only to each other, but to God. He has promised blessings to those who honor that covenant.

EZRA TAFT BENSON

Ensign, Nov. 1982, p. 59.

To marry is an obligation as well as an opportunity. Every normal person should find a proper mate and be sealed for eternity in the temple of the Lord. Failure to do so is disobedience and a sin of omission, unless every proper effort is made.

SPENCER W. KIMBALL

The Miracle of Forgiveness, Deseret Book, 1969, p. 97.

What God has joined together, let no man put asunder.

MATTHEW 19:6

Marriage is the closest and most intimate relationship one makes in this life, and the most serious and sacred decision. If you haven't been to the Lord's house, get ready, be clean, prepare to come to establish the foundation for a special, happy, eternal marriage.

MARION D. HANKS

Ensign, Nov. 1984, p. 35.

Marriage itself must be regarded as a sacred covenant before God. A married couple has an obligation not only to each other, but to God. He has promised blessings to those who honor that covenant.

EZRA TAFT BENSON

Ensign, Nov. 1982, p. 59.

God not only commends but he commands marriage. While man was yet immortal, before sin had entered the world, our Heavenly Father himself performed the first marriage. He united our first parents in the bonds of holy matrimony, and commanded them to be fruitful and multiply and replenish the earth. This command he has never changed, abrogated or annulled; but it has continued in force throughout all the generations of mankind.

JOSEPH F. SMITH

Gospel Doctrine, Deseret Book, p. 274.

It is one to wed within the new and everlasting covenant and another to abide in that covenant. One must abide in marriage covenant to receive the blessings of exaltation in our Heavenly Father's kingdom....

When a couple abides in the marriage covenant, the husband values his wife as the nurturer of their children and as a co-creator with Father in Heaven. The wife supports her husband as the provider and protector of their family.

W. DOUGLAS SHUMWAY

Ensign, August 2005, p. 19.

Temple marriages are less likely to result in divorce. For marriages performed outside the temples, the threat of divorce is much greater. In a study of our own groups, we found that there was only one divorce in every 16 marriages of those who were sealed in the temple, while there was one divorce in every 5.7 marriages of those who were not . . . .

Not only the ordinance itself, but also the preparation for the ordinance and the deep appreciation of it achieve this end. The righteousness of your life, the feeling of responsibility in preparation for temple marriage, as well as the sacred sealing ordinance, combine to solemnize marriage vows, make holy family relationships, and cement ties, resulting in a continuous and blissful marriage.

SPENCER W. KIMBALL

The Teachings of Spencer W. Kimball, Bookcraft, 1982, pp. 297-298.

Marriage according to the law of the Church is the most holy and sacred ordinance. It will bring to the husband and the wife, if they abide in their covenants, the fullness of exaltation in the kingdom of God.

JOSEPH FIELDING SMITH

Quoted in "The Family Is Central To The Creator's Plan," *Ensign*, Dec. 2004, p. 51.

Devotion

Thou shalt love thy wife (or husband) with all thy heart.

DOCTRINE AND COVENANTS 42:22

"Husbands, love your wives, even as Christ also loved the church." (Ephesians 5:25)

This kind of love can be shown for your wives in so many ways. First and foremost, nothing except God Himself takes priority over your wife in your life—not work, not recreation, not hobbies. Your wife is your precious, eternal helpmate—your companion.

What does it mean to love someone with all your heart? It means to love with all your emotional feelings and with all your devotion. Surely when you love your wife with all your heart, you cannot demean her, criticize her, find fault with her, or abuse her by words, sullen behavior, or actions.

What does it mean to "cleave" unto her? It means to stay close to her, to be loyal and faithful to her, to communicate with her, and to express your love for her.

Love means being sensitive to her feelings and needs. She wants to be noticed and treasured. She wants to be told that you view her as lovely and attractive and important to you. Love means putting her welfare and self-esteem as a high priority in your life.

EZRA TAFT BENSON

Ensign, Nov. 1987, p. 50.

Having the companionship and enjoying the fruits of a Holy and Divine Presence is the kernel of a great happiness in marriage. Spiritual oneness is the anchor. Slow leaks in the sanctifying dimension of marriage often cause marriages to become flat tires.

JAMES E. FAUST

Ensign, Nov. 1977, p. 11.

The trick, my brethren and sisters, is to enjoy the journey, traveling hand in hand, in sunshine and storm, as companions who love one another.

GORDON B. HINCKLEY

Teachings of Gordon B. Hinckley, Deseret Book, 1997, p. 324.

And said, For this cause shall
a man leave father and mother,
and shall cleave to his wife: and
they shall be one flesh?

MATTHEW 19:5

Responsibility to spouse supersedes even children. The Lord says in definite terms: "Thou shalt love thy wife with all they heart, and shall cleave unto her and none else." (D&C 42:22)

The words "none else" eliminate everyone and everything. The spouse then becomes preeminent in the life of the husband or wife, and neither social life nor occupational life nor political life nor any other interest nor person nor thing shall ever take precedence over the companion spouse.

We sometimes find women who absorb and hover over the children at the expense of the husband, sometimes even estranging them from him. This is in direct violation of the command: None else.

SPENCER W. KIMBALL

The Teachings of Spencer W. Kimball, Bookcraft, 1982, pp. 297-298.

Fidelity

Never turn to a third party in time of trouble, except appropriate family members or your bishop or stake president. When marriage partners have no one to talk with at home, unfortunately many seek a friend elsewhere. And that is where much adultery begins.

It can happen in the neighborhood, in a ward choir, at the office, or anywhere else.

HUGH W. PINNOCK

Ensign, Sept. 1981, p. 37.

Marriage presupposes total allegiance and total fidelity. Each spouse takes the partner with the understanding that he or she gives totally to the spouse all the heart, strength, loyalty, honor, and affection, with all dignity.

Any divergence is sin; any sharing of the heart is transgression. As we should have "an eye single to the glory of God," so should we have an eye, an ear, a heart single to the marriage and the spouse and family.

SPENCER W. KIMBALL

Faith Precedes the Miracle, Deseret Book, 1981, pp. 142-43.

There are those married people who permit their eyes to wander and their hearts to become vagrant, who think it is not improper to flirt a little, to share their hearts and have desire for someone other than the wife or the husband.

The Lord says in no uncertain terms: "Thou shalt love thy wife with all thy heart, and shalt cleave unto her and none else." (D&C 42:22)

And when the Lord says all thy heart, it allows for no sharing nor dividing nor depriving. And, to the woman it is paraphrased: "Thou shalt love thy husband with all they heart and shalt cleave unto him and none else."

SPENCER W. KIMBALL

Faith Precedes the Miracle, Deseret Book, 1981, pp. 142-43.

Finances

A celestial marriage is far more to fight for and to live for, and to adjust for, than any financial or other gain or beneficial arrangements that two partners might have between them.

SPENCER W. KIMBALL

The Miracle of Forgiveness, Deseret Book, 1969, p. 271.

In the home, money management between husband and wife should be on a partnership basis, with both parties having a voice in decisions and policy-making. When children come along and reach the age of accountability, they too should be involved in money concerns on a limited partnership basis.

Peace, contentment, love, and security in the home are not possible when financial anxieties and bickerings prevail. Whether we are anticipating marriage or are well into it, today is the time for all of us to review and repent as necessary to improve our money management skills and live within our means.

MARVIN J. ASHTON

Ensign, July 1975, p. 72.

Successful financial management in every LDS home begins with the payment of an honest tithe. If our tithing and fast offerings are the first obligations met following the receipt of each paycheck, our commitment to this important gospel principle will be strengthened and the likelihood of financial mismanagement will be reduced.

Paying tithing promptly to Him who does not come to check up each month will teach us and our children to be more honest with those physically closer at hand.

MARVIN J. ASHTON

Ensign, July 1975, p. 72.

There is yet another major cause for divorce that should not go unattended: the mismanagement of family financial resources. To pay tithes and offerings while ignoring the balance of Heavenly Father's advice concerning sound judgment in family finances will probably cause the windows of heaven to stick a little bit. The promised blessings will not likely be forthcoming as expected.

ROBERT L. SIMPSON

Robert L. Simpson, "A Lasting Marriage," Ensign, May 1982, p. 21

Be willing to postpone or forgo some purchases in order to stay within your budget. Pay your tithing first, and avoid debt insofar as possible. Remember that spending fifty dollars a month less than you receive equals happiness and spending fifty more equals misery. The time may have come to get out the scissors and your credit cards and perform what Elder Holland called some "plastic surgery."

As part of this general financial caution we encourage, if necessary, plastic surgery for both husband and wife. This is a very painless operation: Just cut up your credit cards. Unless you are prepared to use those cards under the strictest of conditions and restraints, you should not use them at all—at least not at high rates of interest. No convenience known to modern man has so jeopardized the financial stability of families, especially young struggling families, like the credit card.

PATRICIA T. HOLLAND

Ensign, June 1986, p. 30.

The experience of Latter-day Saint families I interviewed points to several principles of handling money:

1. Communicate! One spouse should never be unsure of what is going on with the finances. All but the most trivial decisions should be made together, combining the wisdom of both husband and wife.

2. Expect only what is reasonable. Money doesn't come easily, especially early in marriage. Neither husband nor wife should expect to be able to spend as they did when they were single.

3. Budget! Plan ahead and follow the plan as closely as you can. Record where the money went. Unless you know where you really want the money to go, it won't go there! But be prepared to adjust the budget to meet emergency and unplanned needs.

4. For most purchases, reject debt! The temptation to buy now and pay later must generally be avoided if a couple hopes to be financially secure. Do not borrow to invest in speculative ventures.

5. Remember that your marriage is more important than anything you might own, more important than any problem you might face. Don't let money be a wedge between you.

ORSON SCOTT CARD

Ensign, June 1978, p. 13.

I learned in serving almost twenty years as bishop and stake president that an excellent insurance against divorce is the payment of tithing. Payment of tithing seems to facilitate keeping the spiritual battery charged in order to make it through the times when the spiritual generator has been idle or not working.

JAMES E. FAUST

Ensign, Nov. 1977, p. 9.

Management of family finances should be mutual between husband and wife in an attitude of openness and trust. Control of the money by one spouse as a source of power and authority causes inequality in the marriage and is inappropriate. Conversely, if a marriage partner voluntarily removes himself or herself entirely from family financial management, that is an abdication of necessary responsibility.

MARVIN J. ASHTON

Ensign, July 1975, p. 72.

Just as your religion should protect you against immorality and violence and other family tragedies, it will protect you against financial despair as well, if you will let it. Pay your tithes and offerings first. No greater financial protection can be offered you.

Then simply budget what is left the rest of that month. Make do with what you have. Do without. Say no. You can hold your head high even if your clothing is not the most stylish nor your home the most regal. You can hold it high for the simple reason that it is not bent or bowed with the relentless burden of debt.

JEFFREY R. AND PATRICIA
T. HOLLAND

Ensign, June 1986, p. 28.

Forgiveness

God our Eternal Father ordained that we should be companions. That implies equality. Marriage is a joint venture.

Of course, there are hazards and problems, but these are secondary to the greater opportunities and great satisfactions that come of sublimating selfish interests, to the good of the partnership.

GORDON B. HINCKLEY

Husbands and Wives Fireside, Jan. 29, 1984.

Most couples have misunderstandings but many solve their problems instead of permitting their problems to crush them. Many wives have shed bitter tears, and many husbands have lain sleepless hours, but thanks be to the Lord that great numbers of these folks have been smart enough to solve their difficulties.

SPENCER W. KIMBALL

The Miracle of Forgiveness, Deseret Book, 1969, p. 271.

If every husband and every wife would constantly do whatever might be possible to ensure the comfort and happiness of his or her companion, there would be very little, if any, divorce. Arguments would never be heard. Accusations would never be leveled. Angry explosions would not occur. Rather, love and concern would replace abuse and meanness.

GORDON B. HINCKLEY

Ensign, Nov. 2004, p. 82.

As hard as it is to form the words, be swift to say, "I apologize, and please forgive me," even though you are not the one who is totally at fault. True love is developed by those who are willing to readily admit personal mistakes and offenses.

JOE J. CHRISTENSEN

Ensign, May 1995, p. 64.

The cure for most marital problems does not lie in divorce. It lies in repentance and forgiveness, in expressions of kindness and concern. It is to be found in application of the Golden Rule.

GORDON B. HINCKLEY

Ensign, Nov. 2004, p. 82.

Happiness

Marriage, my beloved young brothers and sisters, should not be just taken for granted. It must be worked at, but realize that you can have the kind of marriage that you earnestly desire and for which you are willing to work. Marriage will require giving and taking; it will mean sharing, because life was meant to be shared. A happy and successful marriage means forgetting oneself and thinking of ways in which to make one's companion happy.

It might be well each day for the husband to think, "What can I do today to make Mary happy?" And Mary should say to herself, "What can I do today to make John happy?"

A happy home is where the wife is treated like a queen and the husband is treated like a king. And so, it is not only marrying the right partner, it is being the right partner.

HENRY D. TAYLOR

Ensign, Jan. 1974, p. 36.

You must remember that you started out with your courtship on a basis of companionship. You husbands remember when you courted your wives that you did all you could to be enjoyable companions to them; you took them out, showed them a good time, paid them compliments. You never though of criticizing them or embarrassing them because that would never win a fair lady, but you put your own best foot forward always, and you did all you could to convince that young lady that association with you would provide for her a loving, wholesome, desirable companionship. . . .

Where is that companionship now? Are you, as husbands and wives, real companions today? Do you have fun together? Do you ever go out together and really have a good time? Do you work together? Do you worship God together? Do you maintain that high respect for each other that you once had, remembering that there can be no real love at home unless there is respect for each other, and that there is precious little respect unless we are respectable?

MARK E. PETERSEN

Conference Report, Oct. 1954, p. 18.

I have long felt that happiness in marriage is not so much a matter of romance as it is an anxious concern for the comfort and well-being of one's companion. That involves a willingness to overlook weaknesses and mistakes.

One man has said, "Love is not blind—it sees more, not less. But because it sees more, it is willing to see less."

JULIUS GORDON

Julius Gordon, *Treasure Chest*, ed. Charles L. Wallis
[New York: Harper and Row, 1965] p. 168.

Having Children

I am offended by the sophistry that the only lot of the Latter-day Saint women is to be barefoot and pregnant. It's a clever phrase, but it's false. Of course we believe in children. The Lord has told us to multiply and replenish the earth that we might have joy in our posterity, and there is no greater joy than the joy that comes of happy children in good families. But he did not designate the number, nor has the Church.

That is a sacred matter left to the couple and the Lord. The official statement of the Church includes this language: "Husbands must be considerate of their wives, who have the greater responsibility not only of bearing children but of caring for them through childhood, and should help them conserve their health and strength.

"Married couples should exercise self-control in all of their relationships. They should seek inspiration from the Lord in meeting their marital challenges and rear their children according to the teachings of the gospel."

GORDON B. HINCKLEY

General Handbook of Instructions, 1983, p. 770.

The soul of the marriage is greatly enriched and the spiritual growing process is greatly strengthened when a couple become parents. Parenthood should bring the greatest of all happiness. Men grow because as fathers they must take care of their families. Women blossom because as mothers they must forget themselves. We understand best the full meaning of love when we become parents.

JAMES E. FAUST

Ensign, Nov. 1977, p. 9.

I have told tens of thousands of young folks that when they marry they should not wait for children until they have finished their schooling and financial desires. They should live together normally and let the children come. I know of no scriptures where an authorization is given to young wives to withhold their families and go to work to put their husbands through school. There are thousands of husbands who have worked their own way through school and have reared families at the same time.

SPENCER W. KIMBALL

Speeches of the Year, 1973-1974, p. 263.

In the October 1942 general conference, the First Presidency delivered a message to "the Saints in every land and clime," in which they said, "By virtue of the authority in us vested as the First Presidency of the Church, we warn our people."

They also said, "Amongst His earliest commands to Adam and Eve, the Lord said: 'Multiply and replenish the earth.' He has repeated that command in our day. He has again revealed in this, the last dispensation, the principle of the eternity of the marriage covenant.

"The Lord has told us that it is the duty of every husband and wife to obey the command given to Adam to multiply and replenish the earth, so that the legions of choice spirits waiting for their tabernacles of flesh may come here and move forward under God's great design to become perfect souls, for without these fleshly tabernacles they cannot progress to their God-planned destiny. Thus, every husband and wife should become a father and mother in Israel to children born under the holy, eternal covenant."

BOYD K. PACKER

Ensign, Nov. 1993, p. 21.

They should be taught that pure love between the sexes is one of the noblest things on earth and the bearing and rearing of children the highest of all human duties. In this regard, it is the duty of parents to set an example in the home that children may see and absorb the sacredness of family life and the responsibility associated therewith. The purpose of marriage is to bear children and rear a family.

DAVID O. MCKAY

Teachings Of Presidents Of The Church: David O. McKay, 2003, pp. 136-137.

Love

I suppose "loving kindness" is a synonym for charity, or the pure love of Christ. I know that it is an absolutely essential ingredient in an eternal marriage and that romantic love cannot be separated from it or flourish without it. Loving kindness is a common thread in all the exceptional marriages with which I am acquainted, and it is the remedy for almost all marital problems.

MARLIN K. JENSEN

Ensign, Oct. 1994, p. 47.

Thou shalt live together in love.

DOCTRINE AND COVENANTS 42:45

Love one another: for

he that loveth another

hath fulfilled the law.

ROMANS 13:8

Trust is to human relationships what faith is to gospel living. It is the beginning place, the foundation upon which more can be built. Where trust is, love can flourish.

BARBARA B. SMITH

Ensign, Nov. 1981, p. 83.

One great purpose carried out by those who come into the temple is the sealing of man and wife in the sacred bonds of matrimony. That purpose is based upon the fact that man and woman truly love each other. That means that a couple coming to the altar should be sure that there is love in each heart. It would be a terrible thing to be bound for eternity to one whom you do not love, but it is a glorious thing to be sealed for time and eternity to one whom you do love.

Let us ever remember that love is the divinest attribute of the human soul. Love must be fed; love must be nourished; love can be starved to death just as literally as the body can be starved without daily sustenance. If that love is fed daily and monthly and yearly throughout a lifetime, the husband's attention will not be drawn to somebody else.

If your spirit lives after death, as it does, then that attribute of love will persist.

DAVID O. MCKAY

Improvement Era, vol. 68, 1965, p. 92.

Too many believe that love is a condition, a feeling that involves 100 percent of the heart, something that happens to you. They disassociate love from the mind and, therefore, from agency. In commanding us to love, the Lord refers to something much deeper than romance—a love that is the most profound form of loyalty. He is teaching us that love is something more than feelings of the heart; it is also a covenant we keep with soul and mind.

Thus we have seen that while a person may "fall in love" with a spouse by emotion, the husband or wife progresses and blossoms in love by decision.

Because love is as much a verb as it is a noun, the phrase "I love you" is much more a promise of behavior and commitment than it is an expression of feeling. "I love you" is a phrase we should be using in our homes much more than we do. If we don't teach our children to use this phrase, they'll be very uncomfortable with it throughout their lives and may not use it very much in their own marriage or with their own children.

LYNN G. ROBBINS

Ensign, Oct. 2000, p. 16.

Love is like a flower, and, like the body, it needs constant feeding. The mortal body would soon be emaciated and die if there were not frequent feedings. The tender flower would wither and die without food and water. And so love, also, cannot be expected to last forever unless it is continually fed with portions of love, the manifestation of esteem and admiration, the expressions of gratitude, and the consideration of unselfishness.

SPENCER W. KIMBALL

Ensign, Mar. 1977, p. 5.

Let the husbands render unto the wife due benevolence and likewise also the wife unto the husband.

FIRST CORINTHIANS 7:3

Loyalty

Our loyalty to our eternal companion should not be merely physical, but mental and spiritual as well. Since there are no harmless flirtations and no place for jealousy after marriage, it is best to avoid the very appearance of evil by shunning any questionable contact with another to whom we are not married.

JAMES E. FAUST

Ensign, Nov. 1977, p. 9.

Being human, you may some day have differences of opinion resulting even in little quarrels. Neither of you will be so unfaithful to the other as to go back to your parents or friends and discuss with them your little differences. That would be gross disloyalty. Your intimate life is your own and must not be shared with or confided in others. You will not go back to your people for sympathy but will thresh out your own difficulties. Suppose an injury has been inflicted; unkind words have been said; hearts are torn; and each feels that the other is wholly at fault. Nothing is done to heal the wound. The hours pass. There is a throbbing of hearts through the night, a day of sullenness and unkindness and further misunderstanding. Injury is heaped upon injury until the attorney is employed, the home broken, the lives of parents and children blasted.

But there is a healing balm which, if applied early, in but a few minutes will return you to sane thinking; and know that, with so much at stake—your love, yourselves, your family, your ideals, your exaltation, your eternities— you cannot afford to take chances. You must swallow your pride and with courage, you John, would say: "Mary, darling, I'm sorry. I didn't mean to hurt you. Please forgive me." And Mary, you would reply: "John, dear, it was I who was at fault more than you. Please forgive me."

And you go into one another's arms and life is on an even keel again. And when you retire at night, it is forgotten, and there is no chasm between you as you have your family prayer.

SPENCER W. KIMBALL

Faith Precedes the Miracle, Deseret Book, 1981, pp. 134-35.

Marriage presupposes total allegiance and total fidelity. Each spouse takes the partner with the understanding that he or she gives totally to the spouse all the heart, strength, loyalty, honor, and affection, with all dignity.

Any divergence is sin; any sharing of the heart is transgression. As we should have "an eye single to the glory of God," so should we have an eye, an ear, a heart single to the marriage and the spouse and the family.

SPENCER W. KIMBALL

Faith Precedes the Miracle, Deseret Book, 1981, pp. 142-43.

Nourishing the Relationship

They join their lives as companions in the special sense that married people do. Whether in the same room or a world apart, they are married twenty-four hours a day. They care about the whole person, the whole future of each other.

With good humor and good disposition and genuine consideration of the needs of the other, they set out to make it a happy life. They laugh a lot and cry a little. They are warm and considerate and thoughtful: the note, the telephone call, the kind word, the sensitive response, the excitement of heading home to her, of having him come home.

MARION D. HANKS

Ensign, Nov. 1984, p. 35.

What a worthwhile and splendid tradition it is for those who are married and sealed in the temple to return each year on or near their wedding anniversary and recall the promises they have made to each other and to the Lord. Of course, this will be in addition to the many other times that they will attend the temple.

HENRY D. TAYLOR

Ensign, Jan. 1974, p. 36.

As I have performed marriage ceremonies for young couples, I have talked with them about their future and the things that will go into building an increase of love for one another and into the establishment of a happy home. There are four specific things, among others, which I always include.

First, I remind them to keep the covenants which they make as they are married.

Second, addressing myself to the young man, I tell him to make her happy. If he will do all he can to make her happy, she cannot help but want to reciprocate and do everything she can for his comfort and welfare.

Third, I stress the importance of clearing up any misunderstandings they may have. I remind them that it does not matter who is right, but what is right. They should never retire at night with any differences between them. As they kneel together in prayer and ask the Lord to bless them and help them overcome their difficulties, the sweet spirit of forgiveness will come into their hearts, and they will forgive one another as they ask the Lord to forgive them.

Fourth, and very important, I remind them to continue to love one another. I tell them too that marriage is not a fifty-fifty proposition. Each must go the extra mile so there is no contention about the halfway mark. They must keep private matters confidential, and I advise them to solve their own problems without interference from family or friends.

N. ELDON TANNER

Ensign, May 1980, p. 15.

My wife and I made an important choice early in our marriage when I was struggling as a first-year law student and she was overwhelmed by her first teaching position. We rarely met in all our individual comings and goings, and our relationship with each other was suffering noticeably. Even Sundays were burdensome as we tried to fulfill our Church callings and catch up on studies and school preparation.

Finally, we sat down one evening and decided that if our marriage was a very important part of our lives, we had better start acting like it. We agreed to completely honor the Sabbath by refraining from all work, including our studies, and to devote ourselves to building a stronger marriage. We experienced an immediate surge in our feelings toward each other and noticeable improvement in other areas, including my grades and Kathy's teaching.

Twenty-six years later, we are still faced with many similar choices and issues. I hope and pray that we are resolving them in favor of the things that matter most.

MARLIN K. JENSEN

Ensign, Oct. 1994, p. 47.

Your love, like a flower, must be nourished. There will come a great love and interdependence between you, for your love is a divine one. It is deep, inclusive, comprehensive. It is not like that association of the world which is misnamed love, but which is mostly physical attraction. When marriage is based on this only, the parties soon tire of one another. There is a break and a divorce, and a new, fresher physical attraction comes with another marriage which in turn may last only until it, too, becomes stale. The love of which the Lord speaks is not only physical attraction, but spiritual attraction as well. It is faith and confidence in, and understanding of, one another. It is a total partnership. It is companionship with common ideals and standards. It is unselfishness toward and sacrifice for one another. It is cleanliness of thought and action and faith in God and his program. It is parenthood in mortality ever looking toward godhood and creationship, and parenthood of spirits. It is vast, all-inclusive, and limitless. This kind of love never tires or wanes. It lives on through sickness and sorrow, through prosperity and privation, through accomplishment and disappointment, through time and eternity.

SPENCER W. KIMBALL

Faith Precedes the Miracle, Deseret Book, 1981, pp. 130-31.

"Ceaseless pinpricking" can deflate almost any marriage. Generally, each of us is painfully aware of our weaknesses, and we don't need frequent reminders. Few people have ever changed for the better as a result of constant criticism or nagging. If we are not careful, some of what we offer as constructive criticism is actually destructive.

JOE J. CHRISTENSEN

Ensign, May 1995, p. 64.

Make time to do things together—just the two of you. As important as it is to be with the children as a family, you need regular weekly time alone together. Scheduling it will let your children know that you feel that your marriage is so important that you need to nurture it. That takes commitment, planning and scheduling.

It doesn't need to be costly. The time together is the most important element.

JOE J. CHRISTENSEN

Ensign, May 1995, p. 64.

Practical Advice

When there have been times that one spouse's feelings have been hurt by the other spouse's actions, most often it was done unintentionally. Our way of dealing with it is to say to the spouse who's feelings have been hurt, "assume the best," which for us is our way of saying, "I'm sorry, I didn't mean to hurt your feelings." It has helped us resolve problems in a very simple and quick way.

Have fun and enjoy things now. Don't find yourself so busy preparing for tomorrow that you don't enjoy today. Too many couples fall into, "When we finish school . . . when we have a house . . . . when we have a baby" . . . and they forget to have fun now.

It's okay to go to bed mad and solve problems the next day when you're both more calm and rested.

Preferably before marriage commit that you will always, without exception, pay an honest tithing. If I had the opportunity to ask a married couple one question it would be . . . "How do you feel as a couple in relationship to paying a full and honest tithing?" Of course, there are many important questions, but the paying of an honest tithe is an indication of so many other things; a couple's relationship with God, following the prophet's counsel, financial priorities and relying on the Lord for help. Many young couples find that financial issues are usually at the heart of many problems. Following the Lord in relationship to the Law of Tithing will become a safeguard and a protection to a happy marriage.

Marriage is much happier when a choice is made to avoid responding in a sarcastic or demeaning way. A thought might come to say, "I told you so," when a mistake is made, or to tease in a mean way and then say, "just kidding." Our marriage is peaceful and enjoyable because we choose to say things to each other that build each other up instead of tearing each other down.

Before you get married take every opportunity you can to "grow yourself." Living away from parents, working to earn your own money, having roommates, traveling, serving a mission, and pursuing an education gives you opportunities to get to know yourself. Self-management gives you confidence and self-assuredness. Those experiences allow you to explore relationships, some that fail and some that become lifelong, but, you've figured out so much about yourself in the process. You learn your weaknesses so that you can improve, and your strengths so that you have confidence in what you can bring to a relationship. You need to understand yourself before you can give yourself to a union where two become one.

Go to the temple often together. It is so comforting and reassuring to watch each other renew covenants with Heavenly Father that are relevant to your relationship.

Keep a record (journal) of your experiences and feelings during the courting and newlywed time. Those sweet, innocent, tender feelings will be so valuable to draw on later in life. Recording your sentimental feelings about his new wonderful love breathes excitement and energy into the relationship immediately and, in the future. As you read the experiences later, your love will be invigorated as you relive the miracle of your love story.

Allow your spouse downtime—to read a newspaper or watch some football. To relax in a hot tub or curl up with a good book. Home is the only place he/she can truly relax.

Do day-trips where you can explore and have fun. Make lots of memories together. Time in the car and away from home allows you to talk and laugh and learn without distractions and deadlines. Even though you feel busy as newlyweds, it will get MORE busy very soon. So just do it! This will provide you with many happy memories (especially if recorded in journals or on film) that will give your love energy for years to come.

Allow time in order to develop close relationships with your in-laws. Even though you have a special bond, (being brought together through this wonderful person you just married), you are really just barely getting to know each other. And be patient, those relationships may have normal relationship-building bumps before you fully realize the new friendships.

Remember that even though you are completely in love with this person, you are still two different people. You have different upbringings and life experiences which can sometimes cause conflict. It is okay to think and do things differently.

Don't be in a hurry to acquire things; homes, furniture, cars, etc. Don't be afraid to live conservatively and be financially frugal. Budgeting, sacrificing your self-interests, and creating a vision together for your financial future are growth opportunities. Those experiences are so valuable in help a new couple to learn to share a vision, and to work together in all areas of their new life together. A couple can learn those valuable lifelong lessons very early in the marriage if they work and struggle together in the financial arena.

David O. McKay once said a couple should learn to live on the husband's income from the beginning of the marriage, even if the wife is working (save, save, save that second income). If couples do that then they never get used to the financial advantages of two incomes. It safeguards a couple from selfishness and makes it easier when children come to be able to make due with what a husband can provide.

Don't postpone having a family. Marriage is joining with Heavenly Father in the creation of a new, eternal family. Welcoming children shows an understanding of the covenant that a couple enters into at the temple altar. Working in concert with Heavenly Father in the creation of new life seals the marriage vows, shows willingness to consecrate your lives to the building of His kingdom, and allows you, as a couple, to begin creating your eternal posterity. (At a more base level, it is just obedience to a prophet whose words have the power to exalt us.) There is nothing more binding to a new couple than the creation of a new life. It is a miracle that only together can you bring to pass. To have worked together to this end, feels so special and so productive towards the attaining of your eternal goals. The spirit will confirm to you how pleased Heavenly Father is with your commitment and will give you really special, satisfied feelings.

I was a very young bishop in a somewhat inactive ward, with a great number of welfare challenges along with family problems, as the ward was made up of three or four main families who just happened to multiply. Don't get me wrong, they were good people, most of whom had moved from Victor, Idaho to St. Helens, Oregon, to work in the paper mill or the lumber mills. There was not a great deal of selection when it came to the young people finding their eternal companions.

Many of them would go outside the church to look for a spouse and in many cases they would bring their spouse into the church.

However, there were several of the young women who would come to me, with tears in their eyes, saying that their husband just didn't measure up, especially as far as the gospel principles were concerned. Their spouses just didn't measure up to their expectations.

It was then that I realized a very important principle. When taking a companion, take him or her as he or she is at the time. Accept that companion for what he or she is and not what you think that you can make of him or her. Love your choice with all his or her faults or attributes as he or she is at that time.

Then if, after the marriage, there is a change, then it comes as a bonus in the marriage, as a great blessing. But if it doesn't then that individual can be accepted as he or she is without disappointment. In other words, young women, just remember that you cannot always change the person you marry, and there will be enough about the partner that you don't know when you get married that you will have to adjust to, without worrying about those traits you do know about.

Thank God every day for your companion. This will help you from taking them for granted.

Don't delay children. In God's plan, if you're mature enough to get married, you're mature enough to have children. The world will tell you that you need lot's of time to get to know each other. That's just a deceptive way to describe selfishness. The best way to get to know each other is as parents. The best way to get closer to the Lord is to do what He has asked you to do. Some will say you should wait until you have plenty of funds. The prophets have been pretty clear that we shouldn't delay a family for financial considerations. I like the following quote, "Are babies expensive? Some folks think they are luxuries. Here at Ingleside we think they are necessities."

Susan, Anne of Green Gable's nanny in the book Anne of Ingleside by L.M. Montgomery, p. 18.

Specifically discuss what your objectives are as a couple and as a family—in the long run. (i.e. "When you meet again in heaven, what will we want to have accomplished to consider our marriage a success?")

Setting objectives together is an important way to define what it means to be a family. You are likely to uncover some differences in your current definitions of family that can actually enrich your unique understanding of the purpose of family as a couple. Once your objectives are set it will become clear what activities you need and what choices to make to reach your objectives. "The secret of success is constancy of purpose."

Benjamin Disraeli, English Statesman, "A Thought for Today" (Deseret News Press 1961), p. 24.

Prioritize cultural events early in marriage (and just because something is on Broadway doesn't mean it's cultural—find things that have truth in them). It doesn't have to be a big, expensive production (although rush tickets often make that affordable). Think even high school, college, or community productions that are happening all the time. Cultural events will set a tone that will invite the Spirit and provide inspiration for discussions about what you want in life for your companionship and your children. The following is a quote from a BYU professor during a lecture on Bach: "It is important for us to rub shoulders with great things because we have to be improved by them."

BYU Honors Colloquium lecture on J.S. Bach: Fall 1987.

Leave the television out of the bedroom. Most of us aren't strong enough to resist the pull of a TV remote if it's in the room. In marriage, you have enough time apart from each other and enough items even in the home to keep you from communicating to add a distraction in the bedroom where important conversation can occur. I've found that a television in the bedroom also tends to compete with scripture reading, husband-wife study, and prayer. You shouldn't have to leave your bedroom to pray.

It's easy to get pretty serious playing "grownup" once you're married. One of the fastest ways to reconnect on a deep level is to "play" together. Think like a kid—which means don't overthink. Come home and try to see how long it takes you to get the other person to laugh. And while physical play can be incredibly refreshing, I've found that it's easy to do verbal play more frequently. Talk in a funny voice. Play with words and their meaning. Change up the way you respond to a question. All this makes your spouse have to listen to you in a new way and will likely remind them that you enjoy them. You're not going to play with someone you don't like. It also can take a tired person and give them a well of energy. Companion your with playing fun some have so.

Never belittle or say a cutting remark about the other person in front of other people. Seems like an easy enough thing to do but there are rare occasions when our anger can get the best of us and we are tempted to say a mean or cutting remark. This goes back to the old rule our mothers taught us, "If you can't say anything nice, don't say anything at all." It has been my experience that this really works!

It's important to have a healthy intimate life with your spouse. Talk as a couple and find out how each other feels about intimacy and find equal ground. It never fails . . . If I ever feel like my husband and I are not quite in sync, i.e., we seem to be at each other a little more than usual, without fail, if we can come together in this area of our marriage things are so much better and easier to handle. It is so important and something we need to be unselfish about and communicate with our spouse about. We need to be able to feel like we can truly let all our guards down with our spouse and know that we can love each other for who we are. By being able to do this we can get close in our marriages and really be one in designs and daily things that come up in life.

Most arguments in marriage are a matter of selfishness. Even if one of you are right, it isn't worth the fight. Agree to disagree and don't take it personally.

Couple prayer—Husband takes odd days, wife takes even days, you always know who's turn it is.

On your wedding day, after the ceremony, have someone make notes and write down what sealer said. It's easy to forget those wonderful words inspired just for you. Also, write down any fun things that happened on your wedding day so you can remember them.

Be frugal. Before marriage talk about spending habits, financial goals and expectations. Money can be a great source of contention. Don't overindulge financially, unless you have money in hand.

Before becoming a member and before marriage I went to a stake conference. A message was delivered by a general authority. It focused on four things to do to keep happy. These elements included; 1) family prayer; 2) family home evening, 3) do your home teaching. The fourth recommendation was to go on a weekly date with your spouse. That was GREAT ADVICE! I love my wife . . . earlier in our marriage when funds were short our date often consisted of going to Dan's to buy a 25 cent ice cream cone, but we have consistently gone on a weekly date.

Marry someone fun. When I get home from work, if my wife isn't home, I feel lonely . . . coming home is no fun if she's not there. I enjoy being with my wife. She's fun. She brings an element of unpredictability that makes my life surprising and enjoyable.

Attend the temple together often.

Put each other first. Be concerned about your spouse's needs.

Set aside time to have fun together.

The better your relationship with Christ, the better your relationship will be with your spouse.

Find opportunities to serve together.

Speak kindly. The only time you need to scream is when there's a fire.

When contention steps in the Holy Ghost steps out.

Respect

Let the husband render unto the wife due benevolence: and likewise also the wife unto the husband.

1 CORINTHIANS 7:3

In the enriching of marriage the big things are the little things. It is a constant appreciation for each other and a thoughtful demonstration of gratitude. It is the encouraging and the helping of each other to grow. Marriage is a joint quest for the good, the beautiful, and the divine.

JAMES E. FAUST

Ensign, Nov. 1977, p. 9.

Husbands, wives, respect one another. Live worthy of the respect of one another. Cultivate that kind of respect which expresses itself in kindness, forbearance, patience, forgiveness, true affection, without officiousness and without show of authority.

GORDON B. HINCKLEY

Husbands and Wives Fireside, Jan. 29, 1984.

There must be respect for the interests of one another. There must be opportunities and encouragement for the development and expression of individual talent. Any man who denies his wife the time and the encouragement to develop her talents, denies himself and his children a blessing which could grace their home and bless their prosperity.

GORDON B. HINCKLEY

Husbands and Wives Fireside, Jan. 29, 1984.

If husbands and wives would only give greater emphasis to the virtues that are to be found in one another and less to the faults, there would be fewer broken hearts, fewer tears, fewer divorces, and much more happiness in the home of our people.

GORDON B. HINCKLEY

Teachings of Gordon B. Hinckley, p. 322.

No man can please his Heavenly Father who fails to respect the daughters of God. No man can please his Heavenly Father who fails to magnify his wife and companion, and nurture and build and strengthen and share with her.

GORDON B. HINCKLEY

Teachings of Gordon B. Hinckley, Deseret Book, 1997, p. 325

Kindness is an old-fashioned word; we seldom hear it anymore. However, it is neither out of date nor out of fashion. It is a necessary element to any relationship, particularly one as close as marriage.

Along with kindness comes goodwill, another vital element in marriage. Goodwill towards a spouse can be shown by restraint. There is a point beyond which you do not go when you differ in opinion, for it would cause pain or hurt to the other. Goodwill is to have consideration for you partner, to empathize, to see the situation from the others' vantage point, to believe that what was done was the best the other could do.

MILLY DAY

Ensign, Jan. 1998, p. 71.

As a youth, I never heard my father speak a harsh word to my mother. I had not found this to be the case with many of my friends' parents. My father's kindness toward my mother made a deep impression on my young mind.

One evening late in the summer, my father and I were husking corn for supper. I thought this might be an opportune time to ask why he had never raised his voice to Mom. His simple yet sincere response was, "Oh, I love her too much to speak harshly to her."

W. DOUGLAS SHUMWAY

Ensign, Aug. 2005, p. 19.

Your wives are indispensable to your eternal progress. I hope you will never forget that. There are a few men in this Church, I'm glad there are not very many, but there are a few, who think they are superior to their wives. They better realize that they will not be able to achieve the highest degree of glory in the celestial kingdom without their wives standing at their side equally with them. Brethren, they are daughters of God. Treat them as such.

GORDON B. HINCKLEY

Veracruz Mexico Regional Conference, January 27, 1996.

Spirituality

If two people love the Lord more than their own lives and then love each other more than their own lives, working together in total harmony with the gospel program as their basic structure, they are sure to have this great happiness.

SPENCER W. KIMBALL

Taken from the Melchizedek Priesthood Personal Study
Guide 4 – Strengthen Your Brethren.

If two people love the Lord more than their own lives and then love each other more than their own lives, working together in total harmony with the gospel program as their basic structure, they are sure to have this great happiness.

When a husband and wife go together frequently to the holy temple, kneel in prayer together in their home with their family, go hand in hand to their religious meetings, keep their lives wholly chaste, mentally and physically, so that their whole thoughts and desires and love are all centered in one being, the companion, and both are working together for the upbuilding of the kingdom of God, then happiness is at is pinnacle.

SPENCER W. KIMBALL

Marriage and Divorce, Deseret Book, 1976, p. 24.

I know of no other practice that will have so salutary an effect upon your lives as will the practice of kneeling together in prayer. The very words, Our Father in Heaven, have a tremendous effect. You cannot speak them with sincerity and with recognition without having some feeling of accountability to God. The little storms that seem to afflict every marriage become of small consequence while kneeling before the Lord and addressing him as a suppliant son and daughter.

Your daily conversations with him will bring peace into your hearts and a joy into your lives that can come from no other source. Your companionship will sweeten through the years. Your love will strengthen. Your appreciation one for another will grow.

Your children will be blessed with a sense of security that comes of living in a home where dwells the Spirit of God. They will know and love parents who respect one another, and a spirit of respect will grow in their own hearts. They will experience the security of kind words quietly spoken. They will be sheltered by a father and mother who, living honestly with God, live honestly with one another and with their fellowmen. They will mature with a sense of gratitude for blessings great and small. They will grow with faith in the living God.

GORDON B. HINCKLEY

Husbands and Wives Fireside, Jan. 29, 1984.

Where the gospel of Jesus Christ is lived—where there is unselfishness and mutual respect and kindness and forgiveness, there can be happiness and love and eternal life in the most sacred of all human relationships.

GORDON B. HINCKLEY

Teachings of Gordon B. Hinckley, Deseret Book, 1997, p. 327.

Only when we love God above all others, as the Savior taught, will we be capable of offering pure, Christlike love to our companions for all eternity.

MARLIN K. JENSEN

Ensign, Oct. 1994, p. 47.

Unity

I urge husbands and fathers of this church to be the kind of men your wives would not want to be without. I urge the sisters of this Church to be patient, loving, and understanding with their husbands. Those who enter into marriage should be fully prepared to establish their marriage as the first priority in their lives.

JAMES E. FAUST

Ensign, Aug. 2004, p. 5.

It is far more difficult to be of one heart and mind than to be physically one. This unity of heart and mind is manifest in sincere expressions of "I appreciate you" and "I am proud of you." Such domestic harmony results from forgiving and forgetting, essential elements of a maturing marriage relationship. Someone has said that we "should keep our eyes wide open before marriage, and half shut afterward." True charity ought to begin in marriage, for it is a relationship that must be rebuilt every day.

JAMES E. FAUST

Ensign, Aug. 2004, p. 5.

In the home it is a partnership with husband and wife equally yoked together, sharing in decisions, always working together.

BOYD K. PACKER

Ensign, May 1998, p. 73.

Friendship in a marriage is so important. It blows away the chaff and takes the kernel, rejoices in the uniqueness of the other, listens patiently, gives generously, forgives freely. Friendship will motivate one to cross the room one day and say, "I'm sorry; I didn't mean that." It will not pretend perfection nor demand it. It will not insist that both respond exactly the same in every thought and feeling, but it will bring to the union honesty, integrity. There will be repentance and forgiveness in every marriage—every good marriage—and respect and trust.

MARION D. HANKS

Ensign, Nov. 1984, p. 35.

A man and his wife learn to be one by using their similarities to understand each other and their differences to complement each other in serving one another and those around them.

HENRY B. EYRING

Ensign, May 1998, p. 68.

Marriage is a full partnership. When we speak of marriage as a partnership, let us speak of marriage as a full partnership. We do not want our LDS women to be silent partners or limited partners in that eternal assignment! Please be a contributing and full partner.

SPENCER W. KIMBALL

The Teachings of Spencer W. Kimball, Bookcraft, 1982, p. 297.

I wish with all of my heart that every marriage might be a happy marriage. I wish that every marriage might be an eternal partnership. I believe that wish can be realized if there is a willingness to make the effort to bring it to pass.

GORDON B. HINCKLEY

Ensign, Nov. 1989, p. 97.

Couples do well to immediately find their own home, separate and apart from that of the in-laws on either side. The home may be very modest and unpretentious, but still it is an independent domicile. Your married life should become independent of her folks and his folks. You love them more than ever; you cherish their counsel; you appreciate their association; but you live your own lives, being governed by your decisions, by your own prayerful considerations after you have received the counsel from those who should give it. To cleave does not mean merely to occupy the same home, it means to adhere closely, to stick together:

"Wherefore, it is lawful that . . . they twain shall be one flesh, and all this that the earth might answer the end of its creation;

"And that it might be filled with the measure of man, according to his creation before the world was made." (D&C 49:16-17)

SPENCER W. KIMBALL

Address at BYU, Sept. 7, 1976.

Unselfishness

Selfishness is the canker that drives out peace and love. Selfishness is the root on which grow argument, anger, disrespect, infidelity, and divorce.

GORDON B. HINCKLEY

Ensign, May 1982, p. 45.

In marriage, the true love of Christ involves unselfish service to our husband or wife.

THEODORE M. BURTON

Ensign, June 1987, p. 12.

To men within the sound of my voice, wherever you may be, I say, if you are guilty of demeaning behavior toward your wife, if you are prone to dictate and exercise authority over her, if you are selfish and brutal in your actions in the home, then stop it! Repent! Repent now while you have the opportunity to do so.

To you wives who are constantly complaining and see only the dark side of life, and feel that you are unloved and unwanted, look into your own hearts and minds. If there is something wrong, turn about. Put a smile on your faces. Make yourselves attractive. Brighten your outlook. You deny yourselves happiness and court misery if you constantly complain and do nothing to rectify your own faults. Rise above the shrill clamor over rights and prerogatives, and walk in the quiet dignity of a daughter of God.

GORDON B. HINCKLEY

Husbands and Wives Fireside, Jan. 29, 1984.

The successful marriage depends in large measure upon the preparation made in approaching it, which is important to our subject of charting a course. One cannot pick the ripe, rich, luscious fruit from a tree that was never planted, nutured, nor pruned and was not protected against its enemies.

SPENCER W. KIMBALL

The Miracle of Forgiveness, Deseret Book, 1969, p. 242.

I am convinced that almost any two people can get along together and be reasonably happy together if both are totally cooperative, unselfish, and willing to work together. I realize that sometimes there are personality clashes which make the difficulty greater.

Many young couples labor and live under false notions, feeling that a marriage contract, and especially if it is a temple marriage, solves all the problems; and many people further think that marriage is a sort of perpetual motion program. Once set in motion by a marriage ceremony, it will never run down. I want to tell you that there are no marriages that can ever be happy ones unless two people work at it.

SPENCER W. KIMBALL

The Teachings of Spencer W. Kimball, Bookcraft, 1982, pp. 297-298.)

In a properly charted Latter-day Saint marriage, one must be conscious of the need to forget self and love one's companion more than self.

SPENCER W. KIMBALL

The Miracle of Forgiveness, Deseret Book, 1969, p. 271.

About the Authors

Top row: Michele Bell, Nicole Miller
Front row: Erika Brendle, Alicia Gubler, Lindsay Gardner

Lindsay Gardner—Married to Mason Gardner, mother of three: Macie, Camden and Ainsley. Graduated from SUU with a Bachelors Degree in Elementary Education. Currently resides in St. George, Utah where she enjoys karaoke, reading, shopping (without her kids), and spending time with friends and family. Lindsay serves as Mia Maid Advisor in her ward.

Alicia Gubler—Married to Clare Gubler, mother of four: Lindsay (husband Mason), Courtney (wife Mandi), Alex, and Ashlyn. Grandmother of; Macie, Camden, Ainsley and Ivie. Alicia works as a secretary at Panorama Elementary. She resides in St. George, Utah where she enjoys decorating and bargain shopping. Alicia serves in her ward as Nursery Leader with her husband.

Nicole Miller—Married to Matt Miller, mother of five: Austin (attends Yale University, currently serving a mission in Taichung, Taiwan), Max, Zak, Sam and Abby. Nicole graduated from The Skin Institute and currently works as a Master Aesthetician at Red Mountain Spa. She resides with her family in St. George, Utah.

Erika Brendle—Married to Chad Brendle, mother of four: Carter, Quinn, Avery, and Beckham. Grew up in St. George, Utah, where she attended and graduated from Dixie College. While there she met her husband, Chad. In her free time she enjoys spending time with her four young children and husband, playing the flute, drawing and interior decorating. She currently serves as the ward activities chairman with her husband. She currently resides in Sandy, Utah.

Michele Ashman Bell—Married to Gary Bell, mother of four: Weston (wife Megan), Kendyl, Andrea and Rachel. Michele currently resides in Sandy where she teaches aerobics at the Life Centre Athletic Club and is an author of many LDS novels and Christmas books. Michele serves as Relief Society instructor and Activity Day Leader in her ward.